I0772551

Table of Contents

No.	CAMPGROUND :	CAMPGROUND RATING
1	DATE :	1 2 3 4 5 6 7 8 9 10

Location : _______________________ GPS : _______________________

Phone Number : _____________ Website : _____________ Reservation # : _____________

Site # : _____________ Ideal Site # : _____________ for possible retur

Comments : _______________________

Weather : ☀ ⛅ ☁ 🌧 🌦 ❄

The campground offered :

____
____

We camped with :

____
____

Our favorite thing to do at this campground was :

____
____

One thing we'll always remember about this trip was :

____
____

If we visited here again we would be sure to :

____
____

Places to remember for the next time (restaurants, special attractions, entertainment, etc.) :

____
____
____
____

Favorite Memories:

Notes:

Insert
Photo
Here

No	CAMPGROUND :	CAMPGROUND RATING
2	DATE :	1 2 3 4 5 6 7 8 9 10

Location : _______________________ GPS : _______________________

Phone Number : __________ Website : __________ Reservation # : __________

Site # : __________ Ideal Site # : __________ for possible return

Comments : _______________________

Weather : ☼ ⛅ ☁ 🌧 🌦 🌨

The campground offered :

____
____

We camped with :

____
____

Our favorite thing to do at this campground was :

____
____

One thing we'll always remember about this trip was :

____
____

If we visited here again we would be sure to :

____
____

Places to remember for the next time (restaurants, special attractions, entertainment, etc.) :

____
____
____
____

Favorite Memories :

Notes :

Insert
Photo
Here

<table>
<tr><td rowspan="2"> No.

3</td><td>CAMPGROUND :</td><td rowspan="2">CAMPGROUND RATING

1 2 3 4 5 6 7 8 9 10</td></tr>
<tr><td>DATE :</td></tr>
</table>

Location : _______________________________   GPS : _______________________________

Phone Number : ______________   Website : ____________   Reservation # : ____________

Site # : ____________________   Ideal Site # : ____________________   for possible return

Comments : ____

Weather : ☀ ⛅ ☁ 🌧 🌧 🌨

The campground offered :

____

____

We camped with :

____

____

Our favorite thing to do at this campground was :

____

____

One thing we'll always remember about this trip was :

____

____

If we visited here again we would be sure to :

____

____

Places to remember for the next time (restaurants, special attractions, entertainment, etc.) :

____

____

____

____

vorite Memories :

tes :

Insert
Photo
Here

  No **4**	CAMPGROUND : DATE :	CAMPGROUND RATING 1 2 3 4 5 6 7 8 9 10

Location : _______________________________   GPS : _______________________________

Phone Number : _______________   Website : _______________   Reservation # : _______________

Site # : _______________________   Ideal Site # : _______________________   for possible retur

Comments : ____

____

Weather : ☀ ⛅ ☁ 🌧 🌦 🌨

The campground offered :

____

____

We camped with :

____

____

Our favorite thing to do at this campground was :

____

____

One thing we'll always remember about this trip was :

____

____

If we visited here again we would be sure to :

____

____

Places to remember for the next time (restaurants, special attractions, entertainment, etc.) :

____

____

____

____

Favorite Memories :

Notes :

Insert
Photo
Here

No 5	CAMPGROUND : DATE :	CAMPGROUND RATING 1 2 3 4 5 6 7 8 9 10

Location : ___________________________ GPS : ___________________________

Phone Number : ___________ Website : ___________ Reservation # : ___________

Site # : ___________________ Ideal Site # : ___________________ for possible return

Comments : ___________________________

Weather : ☼ ⛅ ☁ 🌧 🌦 🌨

The campground offered :

____

____

We camped with :

____

____

Our favorite thing to do at this campground was :

____

____

One thing we'll always remember about this trip was :

____

____

If we visited here again we would be sure to :

____

____

Places to remember for the next time (restaurants, special attractions, entertainment, etc.) :

____

____

____

____

Favorite Memories :

____
____
____
____

Notes :

____
____
____
____
____
____
____
____
____
____
____
____
____
____

Insert
Photo
Here

No	CAMPGROUND :	CAMPGROUND RATING
6	DATE :	1 2 3 4 5 6 7 8 9 10

Location : ___________________________ GPS : ___________________________

Phone Number : ___________ Website : ___________ Reservation # : ___________

Site # : ___________ Ideal Site # : ___________ for possible return

Comments : ____

Weather :

The campground offered :

____

____

____

We camped with :

____

____

____

Our favorite thing to do at this campground was :

____

____

____

One thing we'll always remember about this trip was :

____

____

____

If we visited here again we would be sure to :

____

____

____

Places to remember for the next time (restaurants, special attractions, entertainment, etc.) :

____

____

____

____

____

vorite Memories :

____

tes :

	No.	CAMPGROUND :	CAMPGROUND RATING
	7	DATE :	1 2 3 4 5 6 7 8 9 10

Location : ___________________________ GPS : ___________________________

Phone Number : ___________ Website : ___________ Reservation # : ___________

Site # : ___________________ Ideal Site # : ___________________ for possible retur

Comments : ____

Weather : ☼ ⛅ ☁ 🌧 🌦 🌨

The campground offered :

____

____

We camped with :

____

____

Our favorite thing to do at this campground was :

____

____

One thing we'll always remember about this trip was :

____

____

If we visited here again we would be sure to :

____

____

Places to remember for the next time (restaurants, special attractions, entertainment, etc.) :

____

____

____

____

Favorite Memories :

Notes :

Insert
Photo
Here

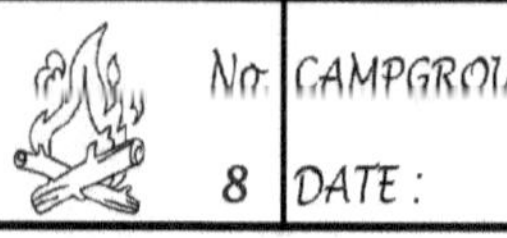

No.	CAMPGROUND :	CAMPGROUND RATING
8	DATE :	1 2 3 4 5 6 7 8 9 10

Location : _______________________ GPS : _______________________

Phone Number : _____________ Website : _____________ Reservation # : _____________

Site # : _____________ Ideal Site # : _____________ for possible return

Comments : _______________________

Weather : ☀ ⛅ ☁ 🌧 🌦 🌨

The campground offered :

____
____

We camped with :

____
____

Our favorite thing to do at this campground was :

____
____

One thing we'll always remember about this trip was :

____
____

If we visited here again we would be sure to :

____
____

Places to remember for the next time (restaurants, special attractions, entertainment, etc.) :

____
____
____
____

Favorite Memories :

Notes :

Insert
Photo
Here

	No	CAMPGROUND :	CAMPGROUND RATING
	9	DATE :	1 2 3 4 5 6 7 8 9 10

Location : _______________________ GPS : _______________________

Phone Number : __________ Website : __________ Reservation # : __________

Site # : __________ Ideal Site # : __________ for possible return

Comments : _______________________

____

Weather : ☀ ⛅ ☁ 🌧 🌦 🌦

The campground offered :

____

____

We camped with :

____

____

Our favorite thing to do at this campground was :

____

____

One thing we'll always remember about this trip was :

____

____

If we visited here again we would be sure to :

____

____

Places to remember for the next time (restaurants, special attractions, entertainment, etc.) :

____

____

____

____

vorite Memories :

____
____
____
____
____

tes :

____
____
____
____
____
____
____
____
____
____
____
____
____
____
____
____

Insert
Photo
Here

<table>
<tr><td rowspan="2"></td><td>No</td><td>CAMPGROUND :</td><td rowspan="2">CAMPGROUND RATING</td></tr>
<tr><td>10</td><td>DATE :</td><td>1 2 3 4 5 6 7 8 9 10</td></tr>
</table>

Location : _______________________________ GPS : _______________________________

Phone Number : _______________ Website : _______________ Reservation # : _______________

Site # : _______________________ Ideal Site # : _______________________ for possible retur

Comments : ____

Weather :

The campground offered :

____

____

We camped with :

____

____

Our favorite thing to do at this campground was :

____

____

One thing we'll always remember about this trip was :

____

____

If we visited here again we would be sure to :

____

____

Places to remember for the next time (restaurants, special attractions, entertainment, etc.) :

____

____

____

____

Favorite Memories :

Notes :

Insert
Photo
Here

No.	CAMPGROUND :	CAMPGROUND RATING
11	DATE :	1 2 3 4 5 6 7 8 9 10

Location : _______________________________ GPS : _______________________________

Phone Number : _______________ Website : _______________ Reservation # : _______________

Site # : _______________ Ideal Site # : _______________ for possible return

Comments : ____

Weather :

The campground offered :

____

____

We camped with :

____

____

Our favorite thing to do at this campground was :

____

____

One thing we'll always remember about this trip was :

____

____

If we visited here again we would be sure to :

____

____

Places to remember for the next time (restaurants, special attractions, entertainment, etc.) :

____

____

____

____

Favorite Memories :

____
____
____
____

Notes :

____
____
____
____
____
____
____
____
____
____
____
____
____
____
____

Insert
Photo
Here

No. 12	CAMPGROUND : DATE :	CAMPGROUND RATING 1 2 3 4 5 6 7 8 9 10

Location : _____________________ GPS : _____________________

Phone Number : ___________ Website : ___________ Reservation # : ___________

Site # : ___________ Ideal Site # : ___________ for possible return

Comments : _____________________

Weather : ☀ ⛅ ☁ 🌧 🌦 🌨

The campground offered :

____

____

We camped with :

____

____

Our favorite thing to do at this campground was :

____

____

One thing we'll always remember about this trip was :

____

____

If we visited here again we would be sure to :

____

____

Places to remember for the next time (restaurants, special attractions, entertainment, etc.) :

____

____

____

____

Favorite Memories :

____
____
____
____
____

Notes :

____
____
____
____
____
____
____
____
____
____
____
____
____
____

	No. CAMPGROUND :	CAMPGROUND RATING
	13 DATE :	1 2 3 4 5 6 7 8 9 10

Location : ____________________ GPS : ____________________

Phone Number : __________ Website : __________ Reservation # : __________

Site # : __________ Ideal Site # : __________ for possible retur

Comments : ____________________

____

Weather : ☀ ⛅ ☁ 🌧 🌦 🌨

The campground offered :

____

____

We camped with :

____

____

Our favorite thing to do at this campground was :

____

____

One thing we'll always remember about this trip was :

____

____

If we visited here again we would be sure to :

____

____

Places to remember for the next time (restaurants, special attractions, entertainment, etc.) :

____

____

____

____

avorite Memories :

otes :

No.	CAMPGROUND :	CAMPGROUND RATING
14	DATE :	1 2 3 4 5 6 7 8 9 10

Location : _____________________ GPS : _____________________

Phone Number : _____________ Website : _____________ Reservation # : _____________

Site # : _____________ Ideal Site # : _____________ for possible return

Comments : _____________________

Weather : ☀ ⛅ ☁ 🌧 🌦 🌨

The campground offered :

____

____

We camped with :

____

____

Our favorite thing to do at this campground was :

____

____

One thing we'll always remember about this trip was :

____

____

If we visited here again we would be sure to :

____

____

Places to remember for the next time (restaurants, special attractions, entertainment, etc.) :

____

____

____

____

Favorite Memories:

Notes:

No.	CAMPGROUND :	CAMPGROUND RATING
15	DATE :	1 2 3 4 5 6 7 8 9 10

Location : ________________________ GPS : ________________________

Phone Number : ____________ Website : ____________ Reservation # : ____________

Site # : ____________ Ideal Site # : ____________ for possible return

Comments : ________________________

Weather :

The campground offered :

____

____

We camped with :

____

____

Our favorite thing to do at this campground was :

____

____

One thing we'll always remember about this trip was :

____

____

If we visited here again we would be sure to :

____

____

Places to remember for the next time (restaurants, special attractions, entertainment, etc.) :

____

____

____

____

Favorite Memories :

____
____
____
____

Notes :

____
____
____
____
____
____
____
____
____
____
____
____
____

Insert
Photo
Here

| No **16** | CAMPGROUND :
 DATE : | CAMPGROUND RATING
 1 2 3 4 5 6 7 8 9 10 |

Location : _______________________   GPS : _______________________

Phone Number : ___________   Website : ___________   Reservation # : ___________

Site # : _______________   Ideal Site # : _______________   for possible retur

Comments : _______________________

Weather : ☀ ⛅ ☁ 🌧 🌦 🌧

The campground offered :

____

____

We camped with :

____

____

Our favorite thing to do at this campground was :

____

____

One thing we'll always remember about this trip was :

____

____

If we visited here again we would be sure to :

____

____

Places to remember for the next time (restaurants, special attractions, entertainment, etc.) :

____

____

____

____

avorite Memories :

____
____
____
____

otes :

____
____
____
____
____
____
____
____
____
____
____
____
____
____

**Insert
Photo
Here**

	No.	CAMPGROUND :	CAMPGROUND RATING
	17	DATE :	1 2 3 4 5 6 7 8 9 10

Location : _____________________________ GPS : _____________________________

Phone Number : _____________ Website : _____________ Reservation # : _____________

Site # : _____________ Ideal Site # : _____________ for possible return

Comments : _____________________________

Weather : ☀ 🌤 ☁ 🌦 🌧 🌨

The campground offered :

____
____

We camped with :

____
____

Our favorite thing to do at this campground was :

____
____

One thing we'll always remember about this trip was :

____
____

If we visited here again we would be sure to :

____
____

Places to remember for the next time (restaurants, special attractions, entertainment, etc.) :

____
____
____
____

Favorite Memories:

Notes:

Insert
Photo
Here

	No.	CAMPGROUND :	CAMPGROUND RATING
	18	DATE :	1 2 3 4 5 6 7 8 9 10

Location : _______________________ GPS : _______________________

Phone Number : _____________ Website : _____________ Reservation # : _____________

Site # : _____________ Ideal Site # : _____________ for possible return

Comments : _______________________

Weather : ☼ ⛅ ☁ 🌧 🌦 🌧

The campground offered :

____

____

We camped with :

____

____

Our favorite thing to do at this campground was :

____

____

One thing we'll always remember about this trip was :

____

____

If we visited here again we would be sure to :

____

____

Places to remember for the next time (restaurants, special attractions, entertainment, etc.) :

____

____

____

____

____

vorite Memories :

tes :

Insert
Photo
Here

<table>
<tr><td>No
19</td><td>CAMPGROUND :
DATE :</td><td>CAMPGROUND RATING
1 2 3 4 5 6 7 8 9 10</td></tr>
</table>

Location : _______________________ GPS : _______________________

Phone Number : ___________ Website : ___________ Reservation # : ___________

Site # : _______________ Ideal Site # : _______________ for possible retur

Comments : _______________________

____

Weather : ☀ 🌤 ☁ 🌧 🌦 🌧

The campground offered :

____

____

We camped with :

____

____

Our favorite thing to do at this campground was :

____

____

One thing we'll always remember about this trip was :

____

____

If we visited here again we would be sure to :

____

____

Places to remember for the next time (restaurants, special attractions, entertainment, etc.) :

____

____

____

____

avorite Memories:

otes:

<table>
<tr><td style="border:1px solid black; text-align:center; padding:60px;">Insert
Photo
Here</td></tr>
</table>

No **20**	CAMPGROUND : DATE :	CAMPGROUND RATING 1 2 3 4 5 6 7 8 9 10

Location : _________________________ GPS : _________________________

Phone Number : ____________ Website : ____________ Reservation # : ____________

Site # : ____________ Ideal Site # : ____________ for possible return

Comments : _________________________

Weather : ☀ ⛅ ☁ 🌧 🌦 🌨

The campground offered :

____

____

We camped with :

____

____

Our favorite thing to do at this campground was :

____

____

One thing we'll always remember about this trip was :

____

____

If we visited here again we would be sure to :

____

____

Places to remember for the next time (restaurants, special attractions, entertainment, etc.) :

____

____

____

____

avorite Memories:

____
____
____
____

otes:

____
____
____
____
____
____
____
____
____
____
____
____
____

**Insert
Photo
Here**

	No.	CAMPGROUND :	CAMPGROUND RATING
	21	DATE :	1 2 3 4 5 6 7 8 9 10

Location : ___________________________ GPS : ___________________________

Phone Number : ___________ Website : ___________ Reservation # : ___________

Site # : ___________ Ideal Site # : ___________ for possible return

Comments : ___________________________

Weather : ☼ ⛅ ☁ ☂ ☂ ☂

The campground offered :

____
____

We camped with :

____
____

Our favorite thing to do at this campground was :

____
____

One thing we'll always remember about this trip was :

____
____

If we visited here again we would be sure to :

____
____

Places to remember for the next time (restaurants, special attractions, entertainment, etc.) :

____
____
____
____

Favorite Memories :

Notes :

Insert
Photo
Here

	No.	CAMPGROUND :	CAMPGROUND RATING
	22	DATE :	1 2 3 4 5 6 7 8 9 10

Location : _______________________ GPS : _______________________

Phone Number : ____________ Website : ____________ Reservation # : ____________

Site # : ____________ Ideal Site # : ____________ for possible retur

Comments : _______________________

Weather : ☀ ⛅ ☁ 🌧 🌦 🌨

The campground offered :

____

____

We camped with :

____

____

Our favorite thing to do at this campground was :

____

____

One thing we'll always remember about this trip was :

____

____

If we visited here again we would be sure to :

____

____

Places to remember for the next time (restaurants, special attractions, entertainment, etc.) :

____

____

____

____

Favorite Memories :

Notes :

Insert
Photo
Here

<table>
<tr><td rowspan="2"></td><td>No.</td><td>CAMPGROUND :</td><td rowspan="2">CAMPGROUND RATING

1 2 3 4 5 6 7 8 9 10</td></tr>
<tr><td>23</td><td>DATE :</td></tr>
</table>

Location : _______________________________ GPS : _______________________________

Phone Number : _______________ Website : _______________ Reservation # : _______________

Site # : _______________________ Ideal Site # : _______________________ for possible return

Comments : ____

Weather : ☀ ⛅ ☁ 🌧 🌦 🌨

The campground offered :

We camped with :

Our favorite thing to do at this campground was :

One thing we'll always remember about this trip was :

If we visited here again we would be sure to :

Places to remember for the next time (restaurants, special attractions, entertainment, etc.) :

avorite Memories :

____
____
____
____

otes :

____
____
____
____
____
____
____
____
____
____
____
____
____
____
____

Insert
Photo
Here

	No	CAMPGROUND :	CAMPGROUND RATING
	24	DATE :	1 2 3 4 5 6 7 8 9 10

Location : ______________________ GPS : ______________________

Phone Number : __________ Website : __________ Reservation # : __________

Site # : __________ Ideal Site # : __________ for possible return

Comments : ______________________

____

Weather : ☀ ⛅ ☁ 🌧 🌦 🌨

The campground offered :

____

____

We camped with :

____

____

Our favorite thing to do at this campground was :

____

____

One thing we'll always remember about this trip was :

____

____

If we visited here again we would be sure to :

____

____

Places to remember for the next time (restaurants, special attractions, entertainment, etc.) :

____

____

____

____

vorite Memories :

____

tes :

____

**Insert
Photo
Here**

<table>
<tr><td rowspan="2"></td><td>No
25</td><td>CAMPGROUND :
DATE :</td><td>CAMPGROUND RATING
1 2 3 4 5 6 7 8 9 10</td></tr>
</table>

Location : _______________________ GPS : _______________________

Phone Number : _____________ Website : _____________ Reservation # : _____________

Site # : _______________ Ideal Site # : _______________ for possible retur[n]

Comments : ____

Weather : ☀ ⛅ ☁ 🌧 🌦 🌨

The campground offered :

____

____

We camped with :

____

____

Our favorite thing to do at this campground was :

____

____

One thing we'll always remember about this trip was :

____

____

If we visited here again we would be sure to :

____

____

Places to remember for the next time (restaurants, special attractions, entertainment, etc.) :

____

____

____

____

avorite Memories :

otes :

Insert
Photo
Here

	No	CAMPGROUND :	CAMPGROUND RATING
	26	DATE :	1 2 3 4 5 6 7 8 9 10

Location : _______________________   GPS : _______________________

Phone Number : _____________   Website : _____________   Reservation # : _____________

Site # : _____________   Ideal Site # : _____________ for possible return

Comments : _______________________

Weather : ☀ ⛅ ☁ 🌧 🌦 🌨

The campground offered :

____

____

We camped with :

____

____

Our favorite thing to do at this campground was :

____

____

One thing we'll always remember about this trip was :

____

____

If we visited here again we would be sure to :

____

____

Places to remember for the next time (restaurants, special attractions, entertainment, etc.) :

____

____

____

____

Favorite Memories:

Notes:

**Insert
Photo
Here**

	No.	CAMPGROUND :	CAMPGROUND RATING
	27	DATE :	1 2 3 4 5 6 7 8 9 10

Location : _______________________________ GPS : _______________________________

Phone Number : _______________ Website : _______________ Reservation # : _______________

Site # : _______________________ Ideal Site # : _______________________ for possible return

Comments : _______________________________

Weather : ☀ ⛅ ☁ 🌧 🌦 🌦

The campground offered :

____

____

We camped with :

____

____

Our favorite thing to do at this campground was :

____

____

One thing we'll always remember about this trip was :

____

____

If we visited here again we would be sure to :

____

____

Places to remember for the next time (restaurants, special attractions, entertainment, etc.) :

____

____

____

____

Favorite Memories :

Notes :

**Insert
Photo
Here**

No. 28	CAMPGROUND : DATE :	CAMPGROUND RATING 1 2 3 4 5 6 7 8 9 10

Location : _______________________ GPS : _______________________

Phone Number : _____________ Website : _____________ Reservation # : _____________

Site # : _______________ Ideal Site # : _______________ for possible retur

Comments : ____

Weather :

The campground offered :

____

____

We camped with :

____

____

Our favorite thing to do at this campground was :

____

____

One thing we'll always remember about this trip was :

____

____

If we visited here again we would be sure to :

____

____

Places to remember for the next time (restaurants, special attractions, entertainment, etc.) :

____

____

____

____

Favorite Memories :

Notes :

Insert
Photo
Here

| No. | CAMPGROUND : | CAMPGROUND RATING |
| 29 | DATE : | 1 2 3 4 5 6 7 8 9 10 |

Location : _______________________   GPS : _______________________

Phone Number : __________   Website : __________   Reservation # : __________

Site # : __________   Ideal Site # : __________   for possible return

Comments : _______________________

Weather :

The campground offered :

____

____

We camped with :

____

____

Our favorite thing to do at this campground was :

____

____

One thing we'll always remember about this trip was :

____

____

If we visited here again we would be sure to :

____

____

Places to remember for the next time (restaurants, special attractions, entertainment, etc.) :

____

____

____

____

Favorite Memories:

Notes:

**Insert
Photo
Here**

<table>
<tr><td rowspan="2"></td><td>N̲o̲</td><td>CAMPGROUND :</td><td>CAMPGROUND RATING</td></tr>
<tr><td>30</td><td>DATE :</td><td>1 2 3 4 5 6 7 8 9 10</td></tr>
</table>

Location : ________________________________ GPS : ________________________________

Phone Number : _______________ Website : _____________ Reservation # : _______________

Site # : ____________________ Ideal Site # : ____________________ for possible return

Comments : ____

____

Weather : ☀ ⛅ ☁ 🌧 🌦 🌨

The campground offered :

____

____

We camped with :

____

____

Our favorite thing to do at this campground was :

____

____

One thing we'll always remember about this trip was :

____

____

If we visited here again we would be sure to :

____

____

Places to remember for the next time (restaurants, special attractions, entertainment, etc.) :

____

____

____

____

Favorite Memories :

Notes :

**Insert
Photo
Here**

<table>
<tr><td>No
31</td><td>CAMPGROUND :
DATE :</td><td>CAMPGROUND RATING
1 2 3 4 5 6 7 8 9 10</td></tr>
</table>

Location : _______________________________ GPS : _______________________________

Phone Number : _____________ Website : _____________ Reservation # : _____________

Site # : _____________________ Ideal Site # : _____________________ for possible return

Comments : _______________________________

Weather : ☀ ⛅ ☁ 🌧 🌦 ❄

The campground offered :

____

____

We camped with :

____

____

Our favorite thing to do at this campground was :

____

____

One thing we'll always remember about this trip was :

____

____

If we visited here again we would be sure to :

____

____

Places to remember for the next time (restaurants, special attractions, entertainment, etc.) :

____

____

____

____

Favorite Memories :

Notes :

**Insert
Photo
Here**

	No	CAMPGROUND :	CAMPGROUND RATING
	32	DATE :	1 2 3 4 5 6 7 8 9 10

Location : _______________________   GPS : _______________________

Phone Number : ___________   Website : ___________   Reservation # : ___________

Site # : ___________   Ideal Site # : ___________   for possible return

Comments : _______________________

Weather : ☀ ⛅ ☁ 🌧 🌦 🌨

The campground offered :

____

____

We camped with :

____

____

Our favorite thing to do at this campground was :

____

____

One thing we'll always remember about this trip was :

____

____

If we visited here again we would be sure to :

____

____

Places to remember for the next time (restaurants, special attractions, entertainment, etc.) :

____

____

____

____

avorite Memories :

otes :

Insert
Photo
Here

No. 33	CAMPGROUND :	CAMPGROUND RATING
	DATE :	1 2 3 4 5 6 7 8 9 10

Location : ___________________________ GPS : ___________________________

Phone Number : ___________ Website : ___________ Reservation # : ___________

Site # : ___________ Ideal Site # : ___________ for possible return

Comments : ___________________________

____

Weather : ☀ ⛅ ☁ 🌧 🌦 🌧

The campground offered :

____

____

We camped with :

____

____

Our favorite thing to do at this campground was :

____

____

One thing we'll always remember about this trip was :

____

____

If we visited here again we would be sure to :

____

____

Places to remember for the next time (restaurants, special attractions, entertainment, etc.) :

____

____

____

____

Favorite Memories :

Notes :

Insert
Photo
Here

<table>
<tr><td></td><td>No.
34</td><td>CAMPGROUND :
DATE :</td><td>CAMPGROUND RATING
1 2 3 4 5 6 7 8 9 10</td></tr>
</table>

Location : _______________________ GPS : _______________________

Phone Number : ____________ Website : __________ Reservation # : __________

Site # : ______________ Ideal Site # : ______________ for possible return

Comments : _______________________

____

Weather : ☼ ⛅ ☁ 🌧 🌨 🌧

The campground offered :

____

____

We camped with :

____

____

Our favorite thing to do at this campground was :

____

____

One thing we'll always remember about this trip was :

____

____

If we visited here again we would be sure to :

____

____

Places to remember for the next time (restaurants, special attractions, entertainment, etc.) :

____

____

____

____

Favorite Memories :

____
____
____
____

Notes :

____
____
____
____
____
____
____
____
____
____
____
____
____
____

No 35	CAMPGROUND :	CAMPGROUND RATING
	DATE :	1 2 3 4 5 6 7 8 9 10

Location : ___________________________ GPS : ___________________________

Phone Number : ___________ Website : ___________ Reservation # : ___________

Site # : ___________ Ideal Site # : ___________ for possible return

Comments : ___________________________

Weather : ☼ ⛅ ☁ 🌧 🌦 🌨

The campground offered :

____
____

We camped with :

____
____

Our favorite thing to do at this campground was :

____
____

One thing we'll always remember about this trip was :

____
____

If we visited here again we would be sure to :

____
____

Places to remember for the next time (restaurants, special attractions, entertainment, etc.) :

____
____
____
____

Favorite Memories:

Notes:

| | No **36** | CAMPGROUND :
 DATE : | CAMPGROUND RATING
 1 2 3 4 5 6 7 8 9 10 |

Location : _______________________ GPS : _______________________

Phone Number : ___________ Website : ___________ Reservation # : ___________

Site # : ___________ Ideal Site # : ___________ for possible return

Comments : _______________________

Weather : ☀ ⛅ ☁ 🌧 🌦 🌨

The campground offered :

____

____

We camped with :

____

____

Our favorite thing to do at this campground was :

____

____

One thing we'll always remember about this trip was :

____

____

If we visited here again we would be sure to :

____

____

Places to remember for the next time (restaurants, special attractions, entertainment, etc.) :

____

____

____

____

Favorite Memories :

____

Notes :

____

Insert
Photo
Here

No.	CAMPGROUND :	CAMPGROUND RATING
37	DATE :	1 2 3 4 5 6 7 8 9 10

Location : _______________________ GPS : _______________________

Phone Number : _____________ Website : _____________ Reservation # : _____________

Site # : _______________ Ideal Site # : _______________ for possible return

Comments : _______________________

Weather : ☀ ⛅ ☁ 🌧 🌦 🌨

The campground offered :

____

____

We camped with :

____

____

Our favorite thing to do at this campground was :

____

____

One thing we'll always remember about this trip was :

____

____

If we visited here again we would be sure to :

____

____

Places to remember for the next time (restaurants, special attractions, entertainment, etc.) :

____

____

____

____

Favorite Memories :

Notes :

**Insert
Photo
Here**

No.	CAMPGROUND :	CAMPGROUND RATING
38	DATE :	1 2 3 4 5 6 7 8 9 10

Location : _______________________________ GPS : _______________________________

Phone Number : ______________ Website : ____________ Reservation # : ______________

Site # : ___________________ Ideal Site # : __________________ for possible return

Comments : ____

Weather : ☀ ⛅ ☁ 🌧 🌦 🌧

The campground offered :

____

____

____

We camped with :

____

____

____

Our favorite thing to do at this campground was :

____

____

____

One thing we'll always remember about this trip was :

____

____

____

If we visited here again we would be sure to :

____

____

____

Places to remember for the next time (restaurants, special attractions, entertainment, etc.) :

____

____

____

____

____

Favorite Memories:

____
____
____
____

Notes:

____
____
____
____
____
____
____
____
____
____
____
____
____
____
____
____
____

No.	CAMPGROUND :	CAMPGROUND RATING
39	DATE :	1 2 3 4 5 6 7 8 9 10

Location : ___________________________ GPS : ___________________________

Phone Number : ___________ Website : ___________ Reservation # : ___________

Site # : ___________ Ideal Site # : ___________ for possible return

Comments : ___________________________

Weather : ☀ ⛅ ☁ 🌧 🌧 🌧

The campground offered :

____

____

We camped with :

____

____

Our favorite thing to do at this campground was :

____

____

One thing we'll always remember about this trip was :

____

____

If we visited here again we would be sure to :

____

____

Places to remember for the next time (restaurants, special attractions, entertainment, etc.) :

____

____

____

____

vorite Memories :

____

____

____

____

tes :

____

____

____

____

____

____

____

____

____

____

____

____

____

____

Insert
Photo
Here

<table>
<tr><td>No
40</td><td>CAMPGROUND :
DATE :</td><td>CAMPGROUND RATING
1 2 3 4 5 6 7 8 9 10</td></tr>
</table>

Location : _______________________ GPS : _______________________

Phone Number : __________ Website : __________ Reservation # : __________

Site # : __________ Ideal Site # : __________ for possible return

Comments : _______________________

Weather :

The campground offered :

____

____

We camped with :

____

____

Our favorite thing to do at this campground was :

____

____

One thing we'll always remember about this trip was :

____

____

If we visited here again we would be sure to :

____

____

Places to remember for the next time (restaurants, special attractions, entertainment, etc.) :

____

____

____

____

Favorite Memories:

____
____
____
____
____

Notes:

____
____
____
____
____
____
____
____
____
____
____
____
____
____
____

Insert
Photo
Here

No. **41**	CAMPGROUND : DATE :	CAMPGROUND RATING 1 2 3 4 5 6 7 8 9 10

Location : _______________________________ GPS : _______________________________

Phone Number : _______________ Website : _______________ Reservation # : _______________

Site # : _______________________ Ideal Site # : _______________________ for possible return

Comments : ____

Weather : ☀ ⛅ ☁ 🌧 🌦 🌨

The campground offered :

____

____

We camped with :

____

____

Our favorite thing to do at this campground was :

____

____

One thing we'll always remember about this trip was :

____

____

If we visited here again we would be sure to :

____

____

Places to remember for the next time (restaurants, special attractions, entertainment, etc.) :

____

____

____

____

avorite Memories:

____
____
____
____
____

otes:

____
____
____
____
____
____
____
____
____
____
____
____
____
____

**Insert
Photo
Here**

<table>
<tr><td rowspan="2">🔥</td><td>N°</td><td>CAMPGROUND :</td><td rowspan="2">CAMPGROUND RATING

1 2 3 4 5 6 7 8 9 10</td></tr>
<tr><td>42</td><td>DATE :</td></tr>
</table>

Location : _______________________________ GPS : _______________________________

Phone Number : _______________ Website : _______________ Reservation # : _______________

Site # : _______________________ Ideal Site # : _______________________ for possible return

Comments : ____

____

Weather : ☀ 🌤 ☁ 🌧 🌦 🌨

The campground offered :

____

____

____

We camped with :

____

____

____

Our favorite thing to do at this campground was :

____

____

____

One thing we'll always remember about this trip was :

____

____

____

If we visited here again we would be sure to :

____

____

____

Places to remember for the next time (restaurants, special attractions, entertainment, etc.) :

____

____

____

____

____

Favorite Memories:

Notes:

**Insert
Photo
Here**

<table>
<tr><td rowspan="2">🔥</td><td>No.</td><td>CAMPGROUND :</td><td rowspan="2">CAMPGROUND RATING
1 2 3 4 5 6 7 8 9 10</td></tr>
<tr><td>43</td><td>DATE :</td></tr>
</table>

Location : _______________________________ GPS : _______________________________

Phone Number : _______________ Website : _______________ Reservation # : _______________

Site # : _______________ Ideal Site # : _______________ for possible retur

Comments : _______________________________

Weather : ☀ ⛅ ☁ 🌧 🌦 🌨

The campground offered :

____

____

We camped with :

____

____

Our favorite thing to do at this campground was :

____

____

One thing we'll always remember about this trip was :

____

____

If we visited here again we would be sure to :

____

____

Places to remember for the next time (restaurants, special attractions, entertainment, etc.) :

____

____

____

____

Favorite Memories:

Notes:

**Insert
Photo
Here**

<table>
<tr><td>No
44</td><td>CAMPGROUND :

DATE :</td><td>CAMPGROUND RATING

1 2 3 4 5 6 7 8 9 10</td></tr>
</table>

Location : ________________________ GPS : ________________________

Phone Number : ____________ Website : ____________ Reservation # : ____________

Site # : ____________ Ideal Site # : ____________ for possible return

Comments : ________________________

Weather : ☼ ⛅ ☁ 🌧 🌦 ❄

The campground offered :

____

____

We camped with :

____

____

Our favorite thing to do at this campground was :

____

____

One thing we'll always remember about this trip was :

____

____

If we visited here again we would be sure to :

____

____

Places to remember for the next time (restaurants, special attractions, entertainment, etc.) :

____

____

____

____

Favorite Memories:

Notes:

**Insert
Photo
Here**

No. 45	CAMPGROUND :	CAMPGROUND RATING
	DATE :	1 2 3 4 5 6 7 8 9 10

Location : ___________________________ GPS : ___________________________

Phone Number : ___________ Website : ___________ Reservation # : ___________

Site # : ___________ Ideal Site # : ___________ for possible return

Comments : ___________________________

Weather : ☼ ☁ ☁ ☂ ☂ ☂

The campground offered :

____
____
____

We camped with :

____
____
____

Our favorite thing to do at this campground was :

____
____
____

One thing we'll always remember about this trip was :

____
____
____

If we visited here again we would be sure to :

____
____
____

Places to remember for the next time (restaurants, special attractions, entertainment, etc.) :

____
____
____
____

Favorite Memories :

Notes :

Insert
Photo
Here

No	CAMPGROUND :	CAMPGROUND RATING
46	DATE :	1 2 3 4 5 6 7 8 9 10

Location : _______________________ GPS : _______________________

Phone Number : ___________ Website : ___________ Reservation # : ___________

Site # : ___________ Ideal Site # : ___________ for possible return

Comments : _______________________

Weather :

The campground offered :

____

____

We camped with :

____

____

Our favorite thing to do at this campground was :

____

____

One thing we'll always remember about this trip was :

____

____

If we visited here again we would be sure to :

____

____

Places to remember for the next time (restaurants, special attractions, entertainment, etc.) :

____

____

____

____

avorite Memories:

____
____
____
____
____

Notes:

____
____
____
____
____
____
____
____
____
____
____
____
____
____
____
____

No. **47**	CAMPGROUND : DATE :	CAMPGROUND RATING 1 2 3 4 5 6 7 8 9 10

Location : _______________________ GPS : _______________________

Phone Number : _____________ Website : _____________ Reservation # : _____________

Site # : _____________ Ideal Site # : _____________ for possible return

Comments : _______________________

____

Weather : ☀ ⛅ ☁ 🌧 🌦 🌨

The campground offered :

____

____

We camped with :

____

____

Our favorite thing to do at this campground was :

____

____

One thing we'll always remember about this trip was :

____

____

If we visited here again we would be sure to :

____

____

Places to remember for the next time (restaurants, special attractions, entertainment, etc.) :

____

____

____

____

Favorite Memories:

____
____
____
____

Notes:

____
____
____
____
____
____
____
____
____
____
____
____
____
____

Insert
Photo
Here

No.	CAMPGROUND :	CAMPGROUND RATING
48	DATE :	1 2 3 4 5 6 7 8 9 10

Location : ___________________________   GPS : ___________________________

Phone Number : ___________   Website : ___________   Reservation # : ___________

Site # : ___________   Ideal Site # : ___________   for possible return

Comments : ___________________________

Weather :

The campground offered :

____

____

We camped with :

____

____

Our favorite thing to do at this campground was :

____

____

One thing we'll always remember about this trip was :

____

____

If we visited here again we would be sure to :

____

____

Places to remember for the next time (restaurants, special attractions, entertainment, etc.) :

____

____

____

____

Favorite Memories :

Notes :

**Insert
Photo
Here**

	No **49** **CAMPGROUND :** **DATE :**	**CAMPGROUND RATING** 1 2 3 4 5 6 7 8 9 10

Location : _______________________ GPS : _______________________

Phone Number : _____________ Website : _____________ Reservation # : _____________

Site # : _____________ Ideal Site # : _____________ for possible return

Comments : _______________________

Weather :

The campground offered :

____

____

We camped with :

____

____

Our favorite thing to do at this campground was :

____

____

One thing we'll always remember about this trip was :

____

____

If we visited here again we would be sure to :

____

____

Places to remember for the next time (restaurants, special attractions, entertainment, etc.) :

____

____

____

____

Favorite Memories :

____

____

____

____

Notes :

____

____

____

____

____

____

____

____

____

____

____

____

____

____

Insert
Photo
Here

	No CAMPGROUND :	CAMPGROUND RATING
	50 DATE :	1 2 3 4 5 6 7 8 9 10

Location : _______________________ GPS : _______________________

Phone Number : ___________ Website : ___________ Reservation # : ___________

Site # : ___________ Ideal Site # : ___________ for possible return

Comments : _______________________

Weather :

The campground offered :

____

____

We camped with :

____

____

Our favorite thing to do at this campground was :

____

____

One thing we'll always remember about this trip was :

____

____

If we visited here again we would be sure to :

____

____

Places to remember for the next time (restaurants, special attractions, entertainment, etc.) :

____

____

____

____

Favorite Memories:

Notes:

No. **51**	**CAMPGROUND :** **DATE :**	**CAMPGROUND RATING** 1 2 3 4 5 6 7 8 9 10

Location : _____________________ GPS : _____________________

Phone Number : __________ Website : __________ Reservation # : __________

Site # : __________ Ideal Site # : __________ for possible return

Comments : _____________________

Weather : ☼ ☁ ☁ ☂ ☂ ☂

The campground offered :

____
____

We camped with :

____
____

Our favorite thing to do at this campground was :

____
____

One thing we'll always remember about this trip was :

____
____

If we visited here again we would be sure to :

____
____

Places to remember for the next time (restaurants, special attractions, entertainment, etc.) :

____
____
____
____

____
____
____
____

otes :

____
____
____
____
____
____
____
____
____
____
____
____
____
____

Insert
Photo
Here

<table>
<tr><td>No
52</td><td>CAMPGROUND :
DATE :</td><td>CAMPGROUND RATING
1 2 3 4 5 6 7 8 9 10</td></tr>
</table>

Location : ______________________ GPS : ______________________

Phone Number : ___________ Website : ___________ Reservation # : ___________

Site # : ___________ Ideal Site # : ___________ for possible return

Comments : ______________________

Weather : ☀ ⛅ ☁ 🌧 🌦 🌨

The campground offered :

____

____

We camped with :

____

____

Our favorite thing to do at this campground was :

____

____

One thing we'll always remember about this trip was :

____

____

If we visited here again we would be sure to :

____

____

Places to remember for the next time (restaurants, special attractions, entertainment, etc.) :

____

____

____

____

Favorite Memories:

Notes:

Insert
Photo
Here

| No. 53 | CAMPGROUND :
 DATE : | CAMPGROUND RATING
 1 2 3 4 5 6 7 8 9 10 |

Location : ___________________________ GPS : ___________________________

Phone Number : _____________ Website : _____________ Reservation # : _____________

Site # : _____________ Ideal Site # : _____________ for possible return

Comments : ___________________________

Weather :

The campground offered :

____

____

We camped with :

____

____

Our favorite thing to do at this campground was :

____

____

One thing we'll always remember about this trip was :

____

____

If we visited here again we would be sure to :

____

____

Places to remember for the next time (restaurants, special attractions, entertainment, etc.) :

____

____

____

____

Favorite Memories :

Notes :

Insert Photo Here

No. 54	CAMPGROUND :	CAMPGROUND RATING
	DATE :	1 2 3 4 5 6 7 8 9 10

Location : _______________________ GPS : _______________________

Phone Number : ___________ Website : ___________ Reservation # : ___________

Site # : ___________________ Ideal Site # : ___________________ for possible return

Comments : ____

Weather : ☀ ⛅ ☁ 🌧 🌧 🌧

The campground offered :

____

____

We camped with :

____

____

Our favorite thing to do at this campground was :

____

____

One thing we'll always remember about this trip was :

____

____

If we visited here again we would be sure to :

____

____

Places to remember for the next time (restaurants, special attractions, entertainment, etc.) :

____

____

____

____

____

Favorite Memories :

Notes :

<table><tr><td style="border:2px solid black; text-align:center; padding:60px;">Insert
Photo
Here</td></tr></table>

| No 55 | CAMPGROUND :
 DATE : | CAMPGROUND RATING
 1 2 3 4 5 6 7 8 9 10 |

Location : _______________________ GPS : _______________________

Phone Number : ___________ Website : ___________ Reservation # : ___________

Site # : ___________ Ideal Site # : ___________ for possible return

Comments : _______________________

Weather : ☀ ⛅ ☁ 🌧 🌦 🌦

The campground offered :

____

____

We camped with :

____

____

Our favorite thing to do at this campground was :

____

____

One thing we'll always remember about this trip was :

____

____

If we visited here again we would be sure to :

____

____

Places to remember for the next time (restaurants, special attractions, entertainment, etc.) :

____

____

____

Favorite Memories:

____
____
____
____

Notes:

____
____
____
____
____
____
____
____
____
____
____
____
____
____

Insert
Photo
Here

<table>
<tr><td></td><td>No
56</td><td>CAMPGROUND :
DATE :</td><td>CAMPGROUND RATING
1 2 3 4 5 6 7 8 9 10</td></tr>
</table>

Location : _____________________________ GPS : _____________________________

Phone Number : _____________ Website : _____________ Reservation # : _____________

Site # : _____________ Ideal Site # : _____________ for possible return

Comments : _____________________________

____

Weather : ☀ ⛅ ☁ 🌧 🌦 🌨

The campground offered :

____

____

We camped with :

____

____

Our favorite thing to do at this campground was :

____

____

One thing we'll always remember about this trip was :

____

____

If we visited here again we would be sure to :

____

____

Places to remember for the next time (restaurants, special attractions, entertainment, etc.) :

____

____

____

____

Favorite Memories:

Notes:

Insert
Photo
Here

| No. 57 | CAMPGROUND :
DATE : | CAMPGROUND RATING
1 2 3 4 5 6 7 8 9 10 |

Location : _______________________ GPS : _______________________

Phone Number : _____________ Website : _____________ Reservation # : _____________

Site # : _____________ Ideal Site # : _____________ for possible return

Comments : _______________________

Weather : ☀ ⛅ ☁ 🌧 🌦 🌧

The campground offered :

____
____
____

We camped with :

____
____
____

Our favorite thing to do at this campground was :

____
____
____

One thing we'll always remember about this trip was :

____
____
____

If we visited here again we would be sure to :

____
____
____

Places to remember for the next time (restaurants, special attractions, entertainment, etc.) :

____
____
____
____
____

____
____
____
____

____
____
____
____
____
____
____
____
____
____
____
____
____

Insert
Photo
Here

<table>
<tr><td rowspan="2"></td><td>No.</td><td>CAMPGROUND :</td><td rowspan="2">CAMPGROUND RATING</td></tr>
<tr><td>58</td><td>DATE :</td></tr>
</table>

CAMPGROUND RATING

1 2 3 4 5 6 7 8 9 10

Location : _______________________ GPS : _______________________

Phone Number : ___________ Website : ___________ Reservation # : ___________

Site # : ___________ Ideal Site # : ___________ for possible return

Comments : _______________________

Weather :

The campground offered :

____

____

We camped with :

____

____

Our favorite thing to do at this campground was :

____

____

One thing we'll always remember about this trip was :

____

____

If we visited here again we would be sure to :

____

____

Places to remember for the next time (restaurants, special attractions, entertainment, etc.) :

____

____

____

____

Favorite Memories:

____

____

____

____

Notes:

____

____

____

____

____

____

____

____

____

____

____

____

____

____

| No. 59 | CAMPGROUND :
 DATE : | CAMPGROUND RATING
 1 2 3 4 5 6 7 8 9 10 |

Location : _______________________________   GPS : _______________________________

Phone Number : _______________   Website : _______________   Reservation # : _______________

Site # : _______________________   Ideal Site # : _______________________   for possible return

Comments : ____

Weather : ☀ ⛅ ☁ 🌧 🌦 🌨

The campground offered :

____

____

We camped with :

____

____

Our favorite thing to do at this campground was :

____

____

One thing we'll always remember about this trip was :

____

____

If we visited here again we would be sure to :

____

____

Places to remember for the next time (restaurants, special attractions, entertainment, etc.) :

____

____

____

____

Favorite Memories:

____
____
____
____

Notes:

____
____
____
____
____
____
____
____
____
____
____
____

Insert
Photo
Here

| No. 60 | CAMPGROUND :
 DATE : | CAMPGROUND RATING
 1 2 3 4 5 6 7 8 9 10 |

Location : ___________________________ GPS : ___________________________

Phone Number : ___________ Website : ___________ Reservation # : ___________

Site # : ___________ Ideal Site # : ___________ for possible return

Comments : ___________________________

Weather :

The campground offered :

____

____

We camped with :

____

____

Our favorite thing to do at this campground was :

____

____

One thing we'll always remember about this trip was :

____

____

If we visited here again we would be sure to :

____

____

Places to remember for the next time (restaurants, special attractions, entertainment, etc.) :

____

____

____

____

Favorite Memories :

____

____

____

____

Notes :

____

____

____

____

____

____

____

____

____

____

____

____

Insert
Photo
Here